GET YOUR PhD DONE

28 Days to Reboot Your Motivation

Dr. Benjamin Newton

Coaching Academics
www.coachingacademics.co.uk

First published 2023 in the United Kingdom
Under the imprint FB3 Publishing
www.fb3.uk

In association with Coaching Academics
www.coachingacademics.co.uk

Copyright © 2023 Benjamin Newton

All rights reserved. You may not distribute or reproduce any part of this publication except under the fair dealing allowed under UK law. However, you may reproduce copies of the accompanying workbook for your own personal use. The free accompanying workbook is available at www.coachingacademics.co.uk at the time of publication. Use the voucher code COACH2 if prompted. The author reserves the right to withdraw this workbook.

ISBN: 978-1-7394278-0-1 (pbk)
ISBN: 978-1-7394278-2-5 (pbk: Dyslexic-Font Edition)
ISBN: 978-1-7394278-1-8 (ebk)

Disclaimers: This book is not intended to support or treat a mental health problem like depression. If you feel like your mood is low and you wonder if you have depression, it's always worth going to see your GP or family doctor. They can explore different treatment options with you and get you on the way to recovery. At the time of writing in the UK, the NHS website (www.nhs.uk) has a depression self-assessment tool that people can use if they think they might have depression. Other countries may have similar resources.

This book draws on Self-Determination Theory. Other helpful motivational theories are available. My use of Self-Determination Theory in this book does not imply an endorsement of this book from the authors of Self-Determination Theory or from any other work or approach that is referenced in this book.

Finally, as with any self-help book, effort is required.

*To Faith,
Love, your action man*

Contents

Section 1:
Do you want to finish your PhD?
- ✓ Day 1: Introduction
- ✓ Day 2: Why Finish?
- ✓ Day 3: Ready to Change?
- ✓ Day 4: Visualise Finishing Your Thesis

Section 2:
Understanding your motivational challenges.
- ✓ Day 5: Introduction to Self-Determination Theory
- ✓ Day 6: Intrinsic vs. Extrinsic Motivation
- ✓ Day 7: What Motivated You?
- ✓ Day 8: Where Are You Now?
- ✓ Day 9: Autonomy
- ✓ Day 10: Your Autonomy
- ✓ Day 11: Competence
- ✓ Day 12: Your Competence
- ✓ Day 13: Relatedness
- ✓ Day 14: Your Relatedness
- ✓ Day 15: Review and Reflect
- ✓ Day 16: Values
- ✓ Day 17: Values Underpinning Your PhD

Section 3:
Clarifying your specific motivational challenges.
- ✓ Day 18: Motivation Barriers (Part 1)
- ✓ Day 19: Motivation Barriers (Part 2)
- ✓ Day 20: Developing Your problem statement (Part 1)
- ✓ Day 21: Developing Your problem statement (Part 2)

Section 4:
Developing an action plan.
- ✓ Day 22: Prioritising Action (Part 1)
- ✓ Day 23: Prioritising Action (Part 2)
- ✓ Day 24: What Are Your Options?
- ✓ Day 25: Review Your Options
- ✓ Day 26: Putting Together a Plan
- ✓ Day 27: Finding Accountability
- ✓ Day 28: Celebration

Acknowledgments

Section 1:
Do you want to finish your PhD?

By the end of this section, you will have:
- ✓ Identified what you want to achieve when you finish this book.
- ✓ Summarised your motivation for finishing the PhD.
- ✓ Reflected on your readiness to deal with motivational challenges.
- ✓ Created a vision board to help you visualise finishing.

Day 1
Introduction

This book is for you if you are feeling stuck with your PhD. Perhaps you are just getting underway with your PhD and wondering whether to quit now before you have even started with your research. Or maybe you have been soldiering on for months and years and are getting to the point where you want to put it all in the bin.

I've been there.

It took me seven years to get to the point of submission. Those were seven LONG years, but I got there and achieved my PhD.

I started my PhD journey with a one-year scholarship and enrolment on an MPhil. Naively, I believed I could complete the project within the one year of funding available. Fortunately, my funding was extended, and I expanded my research scope for a doctorate degree.

My research focused on understanding people's experience of living with pain and specifically, having their pain taken seriously and believed by others. I set out to produce a theory that would explain why some people's pain was believed and other people's pain was disbelieved. The early days were fun. I enjoyed a different scene of work, reading and annotating papers in coffee shops.

When I started conducting data collection, I loved interviewing patients. I listened to their stories of life with chronic pain. I validated them. I began making sense of what was going on.

However, it was the data transcription[1] that was awful. It took hours. Sat in a lonely postgraduate office, with wasps flying around. Playing and replaying the tapes. Typing transcript notation. My chocolate consumption increased and my motivation dived.

I wrote about my demotivation in the reflective section of my thesis. Looking back at this now, I struggle to comprehend that 1.5 hours of audio data took me two weeks to transcribe! I think this reveals how deeply demotivated I was.

Then there was the qualitative software for analysis. I became wedded to the computer to do any analytical thinking. My creativity abandoned me. My free-thinking

---

[1] For those readers who do not know the joys of interview transcribing, researchers who work with qualitative data may record the audio of interviews with participants. These audio records will often be painstakingly typed up to form a written record of the conversation.

stagnated. I lost the passion for my work and I struggled to make the essential links that theorising requires.

Thankfully, I started meeting up with an academic mentor. I discussed my work and how I felt about it. We set specific goals for the weeks ahead. Whilst I cannot say for sure that my mentor saved my thesis, I am sure she played a significant part in helping me through it.

Seven years after enrolling, I had my viva and passed with minor corrections. I did it. And so can you. You CAN complete your thesis!

You will join the many other PhD graduates who have experienced the thick treacle of thinking and writing, and you will get through it. I hope this book plays some part in leading you into a better place with your doctoral work.

How to use this book
I have divided the book into four sections. In Section 1, I invite you to reflect on what it means to complete your PhD. This will help you connect with the idea of finishing your thesis. In Section 2, I introduce the key concepts of Self-Determination Theory. This is an established and well-researched theory of motivation that I hope will be useful for you to apply to your own situation. Sections 1 and 2 are reflective and designed to

facilitate new learning and insights related to your motivational challenges. Don't feel pressured to identify solutions during these sections. These will come later.

In Section 3, you will bring your insights together to develop a specific problem statement. By having this statement clearly defined, you will be set up to move forward and find a solution through your work in Section 4. This last section provides a structured approach to prioritising your problems. By the end of this section, you will have identified a range of options and a clear way forward to solve your motivational difficulties.

Across all four sections, I have broken the book down into 28 bite-sized chapters. The idea is to have a four-week guide which enables you to take a positive action each day towards addressing your motivational challenges.

I hope that as you progress with the book, you will feel a sense of movement towards getting something done on your doctoral work. Having said this, if you want to make faster progress, feel free to read more than one chapter a day. You may want to finish the book over a weekend. Everyone has their unique pace on their PhD journey.

Each chapter has some key tasks in a text box. These are the key questions to reflect on or the key tasks to action. I have put these in a text box to help you identify the most important questions.

As a coach, I use questions to help stimulate a client's thinking about a topic. However, please do not feel you need to answer every question; that could be overwhelming. Instead, allow the questions to stimulate your thinking and focus on addressing the key tasks and questions in bold.

Before you go any further, go to my website: www.coachingacademics.co.uk to download the free workbook that accompanies this book. Use the voucher code COACH2 if prompted.

I have just got one simple activity for you today: complete the task below.

> **What do you want to achieve by the time you finish this book? Write this down.**

Day 2
Why Finish?

One of the first things I do in coaching is to work with the client to visualise accomplishing their goal. I look at the meaning behind the achievement of their goal. I keep digging down to arrive at a deeper level of meaning.

Say, for instance, you started your thesis because you wanted to get a promotion at work. We would explore what "promotion" means to you. Being promoted could lead to more money; a promotion could enable you to work fewer hours; alternatively, a promotion might give you the skills to find a different job.

Let's say you started the thesis to earn more money.

What is the "so what?"

You might say more money means that you and your partner can afford to move out of the pokey flat you have been living in and start a family.

So what?

You acknowledge that living in the flat has been very stressful and put pressure on your relationship with your partner. You have both experienced frustration about this situation and have been reluctant to try for children. Resolving these issues would bring you more peace and happiness.

You can see from these examples that the reason a person starts their PhD can be multi-layered and complex. By taking the time to explore these reasons, it is possible to get further insight which you can draw on to sustain your motivation.

What does it mean to complete your PhD? What will this open up for you? What career opportunities will this open up? How will this benefit your financial situation? What will it mean relationally to you?

As you finish your thesis, certain things will naturally end. For instance, you might look forward to the time when you no longer have to work with your supervisors. Completing your PhD may allow you the opportunity to move city or change jobs. What opportunities or transitions will open up when you finish your doctoral work? What will change for you?

Tunnel down into the reasons for finishing your thesis. Ask yourself, "so what?" Keep asking yourself this question until you cannot go any further.

> **Spend five to ten minutes working through the key questions below.**

1. What are you looking forward to about completing your thesis?

e.g. I am looking forward to being better qualified.

2. You have identified the things you are looking forward to when you complete your thesis. What are the opportunities or consequences that may arise from these things?

e.g. When I am better qualified, I will be more likely to find a different job.

3. What will these opportunities or consequences mean for your life?

e.g. When I have a different job, I will have more time with my family.

4. What feelings come into play when you think about what this means in your life?

e.g. When I think about more time with my family, I feel happy and excited.

5. Using the above answers, summarise the things you are looking forward to achieving *and* feeling when you complete your thesis.

e.g. Completing my thesis will provide me with a qualification that will open doors to other jobs. These jobs will be better paying and have better conditions such as working from home. This will mean that I will have more time with my family. When I think about more time with my family, I feel happy and excited. This insight offers me a strong motivation to work on my thesis.

Great! That's it for today. See you tomorrow.

Day 3
Ready to Change?

Yesterday, we considered what you are looking forward to when your thesis is complete. Take a moment to review your notes on this. Spend some time acknowledging the feelings you experience *now* in anticipating your PhD being done. Notice any energy this gives you.

Today, we are going to look at your *readiness* to address your motivation challenges. How are you feeling about taking steps towards action? Researchers, such as Prochaska & Velicer[2], have identified that change is a process that can take time. People go through different stages of being ready to make changes. Part of the change process that Prochaska & Velicer outlined is contemplation: Thinking about making the change.

If you are a bit like me, you may think about making changes with lots of things in your life. Some of these things make it into the action stage. Some do not get to the action stage, but they make it into the diary.

---

[2] For one of the key publications looking at the Transtheoretical Model of Change in the context of health behaviours, see Prochaska JO & Velicer WF (1997). The Transtheoretical Model of Health Behavior Change. *American Journal of Health Promotion, 12*(1): 38-48.

Yesterday, I scheduled a reminder to get my wife a birthday present - that was important to diarise, otherwise I would totally fail!

Other things I think about changing but nothing happens. This is the case whenever I use the bathroom and see the black mould on the edge of the bath. I would like to redo this, but it is a lot of effort. [This has now been done!].

Are you ready to take the steps towards action? Make an honest evaluation of yourself regarding becoming motivated to work on your thesis.

Don't be worried if you decide you are not ready at this moment. Acknowledge that your honesty is courageous. If you are not ready now, there may be a later time when you are ready. Can you set a future date in the diary when you review how you are feeling about taking steps towards change?

Ask yourself whether delaying taking action is going to help you in the long run. For some people facing major life events (e.g. a baby), putting things off is absolutely the right thing to do. For others, procrastination merely delays getting you where you want to be.

If you decide you are ready to address your motivation, what action(s) are you prepared to commit to doing? What action(s) are you not prepared to do?

> **Write a summary statement of how ready you are to address your motivation to work on your PhD.**

Hopefully, today helped you to reflect on how ready you are to make some changes. In tomorrow's task, we are going to have some creative space making your own vision board.

Day 4
Visualise Finishing Your Thesis

In Day 2 we considered the "so what" behind finishing, whilst yesterday we looked at your readiness to make changes. Today, I want you to make a visual representation of finishing. This is known as a vision board.

> **Make your own vision board.**

Finishing your PhD may seem a long way off, but the day WILL COME. The good news is that each step you take brings you closer to that day. Your vision board shows the "so what" of finishing. It offers you something to look at, energise and sustain you through the days ahead.

It will be a reminder that you can finish it!

As you think about how you can visually represent what it means to complete your thesis and how you feel about this, I want you to consider where you want to put the finished product. Is it going by your desk at home/work/university? Can you stick it on your laptop? Could a copy go in your wallet? Ideally, you will want to display your vision board somewhere that you will regularly see it whilst thinking about your thesis.

There are no rules around how you visualise finishing. Try not to overthink it!

1. Get a piece of paper and some coloured pens. Your paper can be any size. Alternatively, you can do this on the computer if you prefer and print out the finished product. Just don't let the details stop you from doing it!

2. Write the keywords from your summary on Day 2 of things you are looking forward to about finishing. For example, some keywords you might write could be "guilt-free", "time with friends", "family-time", "promotion opportunities", or "satisfied". These are the words arising from answering the "so-what?" questions. Write these keywords down. If you only have one or two keywords, take some time to expand on them.

3. If you are artistically inclined, illustrate your keywords. For instance, you could draw pictures of being with family, having a promotion, etc. If you are anything like me though, you probably want to use a photo website like Pixabay or Unsplash to download images that represent your keywords.

4. Organise your vision board. Make it beautiful and bold. Use lots of colour to unleash your creative energy!

5. Put your vision board somewhere prominent.

Great job for today, well done. I hope you get to admire your creative endeavours!

Section 2:
Understanding your motivational challenges.

By the end of this section, you will have:
- ✓ Understood the key components of Self-Determination Theory.
- ✓ Reflected on motivations experienced in your PhD work.
- ✓ Identified key motivations behind starting your PhD.
- ✓ Started to identify your key motivational challenges.
- ✓ Applied the core components of Self-Determination Theory.
- ✓ Learnt about your values and how these relate to your PhD.

Day 5
Introduction to Self-Determination Theory

Today, we're going to dive into the motivation theory that this book draws on to help you move forward with your thesis. As you would expect, there is a whole array of ideas out there that help to explain motivation. The motivation theory that this book is based on is *Self-Determination Theory*. This theory was developed by researchers Richard Ryan and Edward Deci[3].

There are several key components to Self-Determination Theory (or SDT). These are:

1. Extrinsic vs. Intrinsic Motivation
2. Autonomy
3. Competence
4. Relatedness

If you experience **intrinsic** motivation, then you are doing something for the sake of the activity. According

---

[3] Ryan and Deci are prolific authors. See www.selfdeterminationtheory.org for more information. One of their key early papers is: Ryan RM & Deci EL (2000). Self-determination theory and the facilitation of intrinsic motivation, social development, and well-being. *American Psychologist*, 55(1): 68–78.

to Ryan and Deci, intrinsic motivation is about curiosity, exploration, and personal development. In contrast, **extrinsic** motivation is when we are driven to do something because of an outward pressure, be it a reward or punishment. We are driven not by our own sense of choice, but by something else. Ryan and Deci state there is much research showing the benefits of intrinsic (rather than extrinsic) motivation.

Take a moment to think about your most recent day at work or at study. Can you identify what was driving you? Possibly a mix of intrinsic and extrinsic motivators. You may have felt under pressure to get a report to your employer (extrinsically motivated). Alternatively, you may have spent some time researching different options for a piece of work you found interesting (intrinsically motivated).

> **Spend five minutes reflecting on the intrinsic and extrinsic motivations you experienced during your most recent work day.**

Alongside intrinsic and extrinsic motivation, the other key components of Self-Determination Theory are autonomy, competence and relatedness. Let's briefly unpack these.

Autonomy refers to a person's sense of choice and control: their agency. A person with high autonomy will be confident that if they do a certain action, it will probably lead to the result they intended. They feel they have a sense of agency.

Competence refers to how much a person feels able to do something. A person with a high sense of competency will believe they have the skills to achieve something. This is about the feeling of being equipped to achieve the action that is needed.

Finally, **relatedness** refers to the human need to have relationships that feel secure. It is the sense of connection with other people an individual has in their context. According to the authors of SDT, relatedness can facilitate intrinsic motivation. As a person feels secure and connected with others, they are more likely to experience internally driven motivation.

Over the next few days, we are going to be looking at the SDT model in more detail and applying it to your particular situation.

Day 6
Intrinsic vs. Extrinsic Motivation

From an early age, we experience rewards and punishments. Our parents, our schools, society's justice system all draw on the carrot-and-stick approach. This is a source of extrinsic motivation. It is an approach that seeks to control behaviour: rewarding behaviour that is desirable and punishing behaviour that is undesirable.

We can take this for granted.

You may have tried to reward yourself so that you felt motivated to work on your PhD. I know I did. When I was transcribing interviews, I bought a huge volume of chocolate to reward myself for getting through the hours of listening and typing. It worked at times!

In contrast, intrinsic motivation is when we do an activity because the activity is inherently valuable for us. Play is a great example of this. Children will spend hours doing completely unproductive activities because the activities are fun and joyful, whether this is exploring a new space or endlessly pressing a button on a toy. My daughter's favourite space is the spice drawer, which leads to utter chaos!

Adults will do risky activities like bungee jumping and rock climbing because they are fun and challenging. People rarely earn money from doing these activities; they do these activities willingly.

Imagine writing your thesis willingly and having fun in the process. What would that be like for you? Picture yourself tomorrow, sitting at your desk, opening up your computer and finding great joy and energy working on your literature review/experiment/data analysis? What would that be like for you? Life changing, perhaps?

If you can make this mindset shift, finishing your PhD will be considerably easier.

> **Look at your vision board and reflect on the different drivers you experience when you work on your thesis. Can you identify both extrinsic and intrinsic motivators?**
> **What can you do to increase your sense of intrinsic motivation?**

Over the next two days, we are going to look at the motivators that you experience in relation to your doctoral research and specifically in relation to the challenges you face. Good job for today.

Day 7
What Motivated You?

As we address motivational challenges in your doctoral work, it may be helpful to take a step back and reflect on your starting point. Today, we are looking at what motivated you to begin your PhD.

There's a certain amount of attraction to new things or novelty. Many of us love getting a new car, a phone upgrade, going to unexplored places, trying unfamiliar foods. When we start our doctoral journey, there can be a sense of newness and excitement. We are setting off on something new, thinking about researching a novel area that will contribute to a bigger discussion in the academic world.

As time goes on, though, the novelty wears off and we experience the work becoming more of a grind. The glamour has gone and we no longer dream of being called a doctor.

Cast your mind back to the start of your doctoral work and think about why you signed up to do a PhD.

What was it about the idea of doing doctoral research that excited you?

What drew you to it?

Specifically, what brought you to the research question that you ended up with?

> **Spend some time exploring what motivated you to start your doctoral work.**

Now, reflect on these motivations. You may have identified that the research question was really interesting. You might have dreamed about solving an important question that would help make a real difference. For me, the topic of believing people in pain was one of social justice. This was a huge motivator for me. It represented an intrinsic motive.

> **What intrinsic motivators can you identify for starting your PhD?**

In addition, there will probably be extrinsic motivators present. For instance, your doctoral research may be funded. You might have a particular career path you want to follow that requires a PhD. You could be drawn to the higher salary a doctorate attracts. Think back to what extrinsic drivers were present.

> **Can you identify the extrinsic motivators that contributed to you starting your PhD?**

Was it easy identifying these motivators? Did anything surprise you looking back? Take a moment to acknowledge the motivators you uncovered.

Fantastic work for today. Hopefully, you've been able to think about the different motives at play when you started your PhD. Tomorrow, we will explore the drivers you are currently experiencing.

Day 8
Where Are You Now?

Yesterday, we looked at some of the drivers that motivated us to start our doctoral work. Now we're going to look at your motivation as it currently stands.

There are lots of questions below. I suggest you read through the questions and respond to those that resonate most for you. You may find it helpful to use the questions to reflect on what is intrinsically and extrinsically motivating you right now.

> **What aspects of your doctoral work do you find intrinsically motivating right now?**

What do you find fun and interesting? What engages you? Is there anything that you would willingly do from your thesis work even if you weren't in a doctoral programme? Can you identify 1-3 aspects? These may be different to what initially motivated you to start your doctoral programme.

What do you find intrinsically motivating at this current moment? It might be helpful to think about what you enjoy about these activities. If you love writing references (unlikely, I know), why is this? Is it because you enjoy getting things done? Is it the use of a particular software you enjoy? Are there any general principles or values here that might be useful to acknowledge?

Next, it will be helpful to think through some of the external drivers that are motivating you (or not) to do your work.

Such drivers might include deadlines your supervisor has imposed. It may be the constraints of your funding. Perhaps the task needs to be done before you can move on to the next stage. Can you think of one to three extrinsic drivers that are currently in play? What does this say about you and your situation?

> **What extrinsic drivers are present for you right now?**

So, you have identified prominent motivations that are present for you. Now I would like you to think about naming the specific motivational challenge you are experiencing around your PhD.

Whether you are just starting out reviewing the literature or you are in the final stages of writing your thesis, name the specific challenge you have with your PhD. You may have more than one! Choose the most significant one - or the one that you'd like to address.

One of the specific issues I faced was transcribing interviews. I struggled to be motivated to sit down and listen to the interviews for hours on end. What's your specific issue? How do you connect this with being intrinsically or extrinsically motivated?

> **What aspects of your doctoral work are you finding hard to get motivated?**

That's it for today. Well done for making space for this critical reflection. If you've found it hard going, take a moment to breathe and be kind to yourself.

Day 9
Autonomy

Back on Day 5, I outlined several components of Self-Determination Theory. Today, we're going to be looking at one of these: autonomy.

Humans are autonomous creatures. We thrive in being able to see the impact of our actions. Just think back to a major project or activity you completed - whether it was a DIY job, being involved in a performance, or even a major clean of your room! I bet at some point you took a step back and marvelled at the work you did, even just for a moment.

We see this in children. Infants LOVE cause and effect. A bit of time spent with a young child is all it takes to learn this. Recently, over lunch with my daughter, I made a noise each time she successfully ate a bean. She giggled with life and excitement at being able to elicit this response. She could act in the world and create an effect. My daughter experienced autonomy.

Autonomy involves being able to relate the achievement of something back to the self. It's the "I did that" sense or feeling.

Ryan and Deci, the authors of Self-Determination Theory, note that this feeling of being autonomous actually increases intrinsic motivation. In other words, as we exercise choice and feel in control, our natural curiosity and drive to explore the world increases.

This contrasts with extrinsic motivation, where humans act in response to external drivers. These drivers reward or punish us and so we can experience feeling drawn or repelled by these forces. The nature of such external drivers can make us feel pushed to take decisions or actions because of the perceived ensuing consequences.

Extrinsic motivation does not appear to facilitate feelings of autonomy: we can lose our sense of freedom and choice.

> **Take a moment to reflect on the last time something good happened to you - this can be in any area of your life, not just your research. Were you more likely to think it was down to luck, or hard work?**

If we want to approach our doctoral work feeling intrinsically motivated, we ought to consider the role of autonomy. Doing so will help us increase our sense of choice and freedom, enabling our actions to be rooted in the personal values we hold.

Good job for today. Tomorrow, we will spend some time assessing where you are at with your sense of autonomy and how this interacts with your work.

Day 10
Your Autonomy

Yesterday, we looked at the important concept of autonomy. This is about your sense of influence and impact on an activity being achieved. Autonomy is related to one's locus of control; the degree to which things feel without or within one's influence.

The activity at the end of Day 8 helped you to acknowledge and name the specific motivational issue you are struggling with. If you skipped this task, go back to Day 8 and have a go. It's really important to be very specific about what you are finding hard to be motivated about. You may have several specific issues. Pick the top one or two most pressing issues.

Today, we will explore the issue of autonomy with some further questions.

Trigger warning: If you have experienced past trauma, you may find exploring experiences outside of your control, triggering. Please use your judgement about whether to continue with this chapter and seek professional advice if needed.

Think about your sense of agency. Your ability to control or not control this motivational challenge. Now consider the following question:

> **What specifically about this issue feels out of your control?**

One of the PhD tasks I found hard was transcribing my interviews. If I investigated this closely, there were factors outside of my control.

For instance, I had to attend the office because this was where the transcribing equipment was based. Even if there were things I didn't like about the office, I still had to go there to work. This was out of my control.

Although you cannot control everything, there are likely to be some aspects to your motivational challenge that you can influence or control.

> **Spend a moment reflecting on what is within your influence or control.**

Back to the transcription example, I could control when I went to the office. I could control how long I spent transcribing. I could even, on reflection, have requested to take the transcription equipment home.

> **Think about why these issues feel in or out of your control. Spend some time writing these reasons down.**

That's it for today. Good job. Take a breather. If it was stressful thinking about this, pause for a moment and do something that is relaxing.

You might look out of the window and watch the world go by, or you may simply want to notice your breathing. Do whatever works for you.

Day 11
Competence

Another significant component of Self-Determination Theory is competence, which is what we're going to explore today.

Ryan and Deci describe feeling competent as a basic psychological need that we need to have satisfied. We all need to feel capable of doing the activities and tasks required of us. We learn the skills required to undertake particular activities; we spend time practicing and our confidence grows as we master the new skills involved.

When I turned 17, I was totally excited about starting driving lessons. In fact, I had my first lesson on my birthday. I had a great experience with my instructor, with the occasional hairy moment. For some reason, I never practiced driving in my parent's car.

Despite passing my test first time, I consistently struggled with parallel parking. This is the manoeuvre to reverse into what feels like a shockingly tiny space whilst other road users watch on.

You are on your own and making everyone wait.

Now, from my own observations of drivers undertaking parallel parking, it is not uncommon to make several attempts at reversing into the space. However, my sense of competence with this procedure did not materialise for the best part of a decade.

The PhD process relies on multiple skills, some of which you will be great at: others, you might feel more 'wobbly' with. We can't feel skilled in everything, so naturally, we might need to accept that there will be specific tasks in which our sense of competence is not where we would like it to be.

> **Think about those aspects of your doctoral work that you feel really skilled at doing. Where do you feel completely in the zone?**

Now have a think about the areas of your PhD research where you have experienced feeling less than fully competent. What do you think was behind this? Take a moment to acknowledge some of the challenging feelings you may have experienced when you did not feel fully competent.

That's it! Tomorrow, we're going to look at the specific motivational challenge(s) you are currently facing and how this relates to your sense of competence.

Day 12
Your Competence

In yesterday's chapter, I described how feeling competent is a basic psychological need: it is vital we feel able to do the tasks set before us. Today, we are going to explore the role of competence in the motivational challenge(s) you face.

Some of you may not feel your motivational challenge is an issue of competency. In my example of transcribing interviews, I largely felt able to get on with the task. Sure, there were some minor technical issues that I needed to seek further guidance for, but on the whole, transcribing was straightforward.

If this resonates with you, there may be other factors to deal with in addressing your motivation. However, you may find it helpful to continue reading this chapter because I am going to encourage you to break down the challenge in more detail.

For many readers, the issue of competency will resonate strongly. You may struggle to know what to do. You may experience these kinds of thoughts:

- "This is really hard. I have no idea what to do."
- "I feel embarrassed. I can't do this."
- "I am totally out of my depth."
- "I'm supposed to be a PhD candidate and I can't even do this."

These can be hard and challenging thoughts and I invite you to recognise your courage in acknowledging these. The experience of doing a PhD can be isolating. However, you can move forward.

Today, I invite you to record your motivational challenge and to break this challenge down into its specific components. This will achieve a couple of things. First, it may help to reduce the sense of overwhelm. Rather than feeling overwhelmed at the whole challenge, you will identify the very specific challenges that are causing you difficulties. Second, by being very specific, you can focus on solving the problem.

To give you an example of what I mean, I am going to draw on my own motivational challenge of transcription[4].

---

[4] I know I just said it wasn't largely an issue of competency for me. However, by sticking to one challenge I can keep it simple for the reader.

Below are some of the key tasks involved in the transcription activity:

- Organise transcription equipment
- Find a quiet space
- Work out how to format transcription text using notation
- Integrate transcription process into computer software
- Play audio
- Type out audio with transcription features

> **Write out the specific components of the activity you feel challenged with.**

Now that you have written these out, I want you to evaluate your feelings of competency for each component. This will help you see where to focus on. You could use a simple rating scale such as easy-moderate-hard. For instance:

- Organise transcription equipment [Easy]
- Find a quiet space [Moderate]
- Work out how to format transcription text using notation [Moderate]
- Integrate transcription process into computer software [Hard]

- Play audio [Easy]
- Type out audio with transcription features [Moderate]

In this example, I can see that I need to focus on the integration process of using computer software.

> **Rate the task components according to their level of challenge for you.**

Finally, having assessed your sense of competence, I would like you to spend a couple of minutes thinking about what aspects of your doctoral work you feel competent in. This reflection will help you gain some perspective on the great things you can do.

> **Write a list of one to three doctoral activities you are great at doing!**

I hope this last activity provides you with some balance to facilitate a healthy perspective; after all, you are doing a PhD so you definitely have some advanced skills!

Good job for today!

Day 13
Relatedness

Today, we are looking at the third key component of Self-Determination Theory; that of relatedness. This is all about connection with others: our friendships, our family, our colleagues.

Good levels of relatedness mean we feel loved and cared for. We believe we matter to other people, such as our life partner or spouse, our friends, our family.

Even in our day-to-day interactions, we have encounters with people who are not our friends, but people we may regularly see. We smile at the security personnel, or the shop worker we frequently meet as we go past. We have a connection with the person on the reception desk as we sign into work. These everyday interactions can also form our experience of relatedness and being connected.

Ryan and Deci highlight the connection between relatedness and intrinsic motivation. They state that where there is a sense of security and relatedness, intrinsic motivation is more likely to thrive. In other words, when we feel a sense of connection, belonging and being cared for, we are more likely to experience the conditions that facilitate curiosity so that we engage in activities for the sake of the activities themselves.

Thinking about my own doctoral research, on occasions I felt a great sense of connection. This was often when I was visiting the local hospital and pain clinics, working with familiar people, connecting with those around me. I felt energy, excitement, and joy at what I was doing. This strongly contrasted with occasions when I was undertaking data transcription and analysis. I completed these activities on my own, often in an empty office. I felt isolated and was more often than not bored or stuck.

Hardly the context for allowing creative energy to flourish.

What I should have done was identify spaces of connection in which I did the work that only I could do. Perhaps I could have worked in coffee lounges. Maybe I should have spent more time with my PhD colleagues during this phase.

> **Reflect on the everyday interactions you have had (or not had) over the last week. How do they help create a sense of connection for you? What links can you make between how connected you feel with others and the motivation to work on your thesis?**

That's it. Well done. Tomorrow, we will apply the concept of relatedness to your current work.

Day 14
Your Relatedness

Yesterday, we began to consider our relationships and connections. What thoughts have you had about this? Perhaps you thought about spaces in your life where you noticed connection? You may also have noticed spaces where connection is less present. Today, we are going to explore your motivational challenge(s) through the lens of relationships.

In thinking about your motivational challenge, is there a physical location you associate with this? Where are you physically located most when this challenge occurs? Are you getting stuck at home, the office, the library, or perhaps the lab? Is it harder in a coffee shop or out in the field? Where are you experiencing this challenge the most?

> **How would you rate your sense of connection in this physical location?**

In other words, in the place where you experience the challenge, what are your relationships like there? You could rate this out of 10, where 1 refers to low levels of connection with others and 10 refers to high levels of connection. If you are experiencing this challenge in several locations, try rating your sense of relatedness or connection for each of the locations.

Thinking back to my own doctoral research, I would rate my sense of relatedness in the clinical context "7", and my experience in the office "3".

What about you?

> **Reflect on why you choose this score for relatedness. What do you think this tells you about your situation? It might be helpful to flesh out the rating you have given. Make some brief notes on the quality of relatedness you have in the space of motivational challenge.**

These questions may help you think this through:

- Can you describe the relationships that are important to you?
- What aspects of these relationships are valuable?
- How do these connections help your doctoral work to flourish?

In contrast, some contexts in which you work may be marked by a lack of connection (e.g. there is nobody present). In other spaces where you work, you may feel neutral about the relationships present (e.g. you notice people but do not feel connected to them). And in some circumstances, you could experience challenging connections with others (e.g. relationships with colleagues, supervisors or professors where you have found conflict).

What would you like the relationships in your workspace to look like? What is in your control to change about these relationships? Are there alternate spaces of work where there is a stronger sense of connectedness for you?

> **Write two to three sentences summarising what you have learnt about the link between your motivational challenge and the connections you have (or don't have) where you work.**

Good job! That's it for today. Hopefully, this helped you think a bit more about the connection between relationships you have and your experience of motivation.

Day 15
Review and Reflect

Today, you are halfway through this book - well done! We've covered a fair bit of ground, thinking through the theory of Self-Determination and applying its concepts to your PhD work. The second half of this book predominantly focuses on thinking through your options and developing an action plan to address your motivation. There will also be activities that consider your values and their relationship with your motivation.

However, before we move into action, we are going to spend some time looking back at what you have read and learnt.

As we go through this chapter, please remember to use the bullet points as an aide to reflect on your experiences; don't get caught up in having to answer every single question.

First, take a moment to think about the theory of Self-Determination itself.

- How has this theory helped you think about motivation differently?
- Has anything surprised you?

- Would you benefit from studying Self-Determination Theory in more depth?
- Perhaps you would like to discover other theories of motivation instead?

> **What have you learnt about Self-Determination Theory?**

We considered the important concepts of intrinsic and extrinsic motivation:

- How do these ideas sit with you?
- Would you like to learn anything further about these ideas?
- How did these concepts change your thinking?
- What did they add to your understanding of both starting your doctoral research and assessing your current motivational challenges?

> **How will nurturing intrinsic motivation help you with your doctoral work?**

After this, we explored the concepts of autonomy, competence and relatedness. We explored how these applied to your motivational challenges.

- What struck you as being significant?
- How will this learning help you move forward?

> **Finally, do you have any emerging ideas that can address your motivational difficulties?**

And we're done. Tomorrow, we are looking at the values that you hold and how these may shape your motivational challenges.

Day 16
Values

The last two chapters in this section are concerned with values. Today, we will explore the impact that values have on our motivation.

So, what are values? Values are principles and ideals that are important to us. They can be individual and personal to us. There are many examples of values; too many to list! Some values I hold include clarity, freedom, and justice.

Values come in many shapes and sizes. They are personal to us. The things that we value will differ from the things that other people value. We may find that people close to us share similar values, but of course, even our nearest and dearest can have different values, or at least, different ways of putting these values into practice: Both my spouse and I value a tidy house, but she values this more when friends are coming round, whereas I value it all the time!

The values we hold appear to be stable. We don't frequently change our values. They seem to be consistent. It would be quite odd to go from being somebody who holds a value of justice one day to acting in a way that appears unjust another day. Of course, we can act in inconsistent ways, but this is unlikely to be because our values suddenly change.

Sometimes our motivational challenges can arise because of a conflict in values. We may find ourselves in a situation where there are competing values and we feel uncertain how to proceed. For instance, in some work places, there have been times when others have asked me to do things I felt uncomfortable doing. Whilst I valued the relationship with my superiors, I also valued my sense of integrity. In these types of scenarios, I have felt stuck and unsure how to move forward.

One way we can identify our values is by reflecting on how we use our resources. What have we invested our time and money in? Where do we put our energy and focus? What are the underlying values behind this?

> **Take a moment to think about your values.**
> **What is really important to you?**

An alternative approach to discovering your values is to dig deeper into the reasons 'why' you did something. We already considered this approach on Day 2, when I suggested an activity that encouraged you to reflect on why you want to complete your thesis.

Through repeatedly asking "why", you will eventually be able to identify the core values in play. You can use this approach to explore the values underpinning choices and behaviour.

Several years ago, I used to be a volunteer debt adviser and would spend my evenings meeting with clients. What follows is an example of using the "why" questions to uncover my values at work here.

Why did I do this volunteering?
I enjoyed helping clients manage their debt and feel more in control of their finances.

Why did I enjoy this?
I enjoyed making a difference in their lives.

Why? What does this say about my values?
I value social justice and freedom.

By digging deeper into the reasons behind your choices or behaviours and asking why, you can discover the values you hold.

> **Think through 3 situations in which you did something specific. Using the "why" questions, try to identify the underlying values in play.**

You could start with something outside of your doctoral research, for instance, in your home or leisure. Perhaps start with something fun. Tomorrow, we can look at applying this to your doctoral work. That's it for today, well done.

Day 17
Values Underpinning Your PhD

Yesterday, we looked at what values are and did a quick dive into some values you hold. Take a quick look back at your reflections in the previous chapter to remind yourself about them. How do these values relate to your doctoral research?

Thinking back to the values I held when I was working on my doctorate, I strongly valued relationships with others, particularly time with other people. I can see that when I felt isolated doing PhD data analysis and writing up my thesis, this contrasted with my value of time with others. No wonder I experienced being drawn away from work on my thesis!

If you can make links to what your values are and how they relate to your doctoral research, you may spot a connection with your motivational challenge. Think about the following statement:

When I sit down to do my doctoral work, I think "I would rather be doing…"

What would you rather be doing instead of doing your doctoral work? Time with friends? Shopping? Checking social media? Having a beer?

What values might your response to the above show? To gain insight into your values, ask yourself why you would rather be doing this activity than your doctoral work. What does this activity achieve? Why is this important to you?

Next, let's think through the values behind why you started your doctoral research. Look at your reflections on Day 7 if this helps. What drew you to start a PhD? Why did it seem a good idea? What does this say about you and the values you hold? This, of course, may be multi-faceted. Keep asking yourself "why" to identify your underlying values.

There were several reasons that I was drawn to start doctoral research. I previously concluded that Clinical Psychology was not a career path for me and one of my former supervisors had suggested I consider a PhD programme. I loved research and enjoyed thinking through complex ideas. When I had been in a job for a couple of years, I started looking at other possibilities and discovered a funded doctoral programme.

Some of my other values at the time included thinking critically. The choice of topic was partly determined by my value for social justice: I looked at people's experiences of being disbelieved with chronic pain.

Of course, not everything we do springs from closely held values, but for me, the key value for choosing the doctoral topic was social justice. It was actually this value that sustained me through some rocky times of low motivation and wanting to abandon it all. I kept on with my research because I wanted the voices and stories of people I interviewed to be heard. What about you?

> **What are some of the key values and factors for you in starting your doctoral work? How do these inform the intrinsic and extrinsic motivators you identified on Day 7?**

Hopefully, you found today thought provoking. In tomorrow's chapter, we are going to look at the barriers that impede your motivation.

Section 3:
Clarifying your specific motivational challenges.

By the end of this section, you will have:
- ✓ Gained insight into your motivational barriers.
- ✓ Developed a specific problem statement summarising your challenges.

Day 18
Motivation Barriers (Part 1)

Over the next two days, we are going to review all your hard reflections and identify your key motivational barriers. By the end of tomorrow, you will have a clear sense of what is hindering you from completing your thesis.

A word of caution; try to avoid jumping into finding solutions. We will explore your options in later chapters. If you have ideas about how to solve these, find a place to write them down and acknowledge them without jumping into problem solving (unless, of course, it's an immediate urgent issue!).

Let's start with thinking about why you started your PhD, which we considered on Day 7. Recall we talked about the difference between intrinsic and extrinsic motivation? Can you determine what intrinsic motivators were present when you started your doctoral work (e.g. curiosity in the PhD topic)? You may also identify extrinsic motivators at the start of your PhD (e.g. you were offered a scholarship). Write down any intrinsic and extrinsic motivators.

As time passes, things can change for us. This can include our motivation. Consider whether the motivation for doing your work at the start of your PhD is the same motivation that is present for you now.

For example, imagine for a moment a PhD student called Vinod was studying pollution in the English Channel and he was drawn to this topic because he wanted to highlight environmental issues through his research. He still feels passionate about this topic, however he has recently faced challenges with his data collection and this is contributing to him feeling demotivated.

In this example, Vinod was intrinsically motivated to study his PhD topic and this intrinsic interest continues. The problem he experiences stems from a blockage in his work. He needs to focus on resolving the barriers to data collection.

Imagine a different scenario where the starting motivation was more extrinsic. For instance, a PhD student called Beth embarked on her doctoral research following her undergraduate degree. She could see the path as leading to a higher salary. However, now she is in the middle of writing her thesis, the idea of earning more money no longer appeals. Instead, she would rather spend more time with her friends than stay up late typing. In this situation, the initial motivation is no longer present and she may need to find a different source of motivation to sustain her.

> **Reflect on how your motivation to work on your PhD has changed. How might this be a barrier to your work?**

Finally, let's think about the connection between your values and your motivation. We considered this in yesterday's chapter. Imagine one of your values is novelty. You initially loved the new experience of the PhD programme and the change this represented from a 9-5 job. However, having completed two years of work, your experience of novelty is now fading. We can see that a key value that was present at the start of the PhD is no longer being experienced. Spend some time assessing how present (or absent) the values that motivated you to start the doctoral work are for you now.

> **What role do values play in the motivational barriers you face?**

Good job for today. If it helps, take a moment to check in with yourself how you're doing. Do you need to create a brief pause in your day for self-care?

Day 19
Motivation Barriers (Part 2)

In this chapter, we will continue to identify motivational barriers to your doctoral research. Yesterday, we looked at the intrinsic and extrinsic motivators behind you starting your thesis. We considered how your values interacted with your motivation. Today, we will focus on autonomy, competence, and relatedness, to understand your motivational barriers.

First, let's consider autonomy. This is the sense of being in control and making things happen. I suggest you revisit your reflections in Days 9 & 10 to recap on what you identified. I invite you to consider your motivational challenges in relation to autonomy. What aspects of your doctoral work feel out of your control? Why do you think this presents a problem? This may include your supervisor surprising you with unachievable deadlines. It might be your health means you have days you cannot work. Or there may be constraints on being able to access the research lab.

If thinking about things that are out of your control is triggering for you, practice some self-care and, if necessary, seek professional help.

> **What aspects of your doctoral work feel out of your control and impact your desire to work?**

Second, let's reflect on the role of competency; that sense of feeling capable. Again, I recommend revisiting your answers to the questions in Days 11 & 12. I invite you to identify key motivational barriers associated with any feeling of being deficient in competency.

Remember, when we are looking at your feeling of competency, we are not automatically referring to an actual skill deficit. You may, in fact, be more than capable of a particular task or skill. Rather, this is about your *feeling* of competency, which may or may not have a factual basis.

So, what role does competence play in the motivational challenges you face?

> **How does your sense of competency impact your motivation?**

Finally, we will consider relatedness. This is the sense of having connections with others; the feeling that we matter and are loved. Look back at Days 13 and 14 for a refresher of what you wrote. When we consider our motivational barriers, the role of connection can play a key part. Think about the specific contexts in which you undertake your doctoral work. What is your sense of connection with others in these places? How does this impact your motivation?

> **What motivational barriers does relatedness help you identify?**

Now that you have gone through this review, list the motivational barriers you have identified. Your list might look something like this:

1. I am no longer motivated by a six-figure salary. (Initial motivation)
2. I value novelty, but the research I am doing now feels boring and familiar. (Value)
3. Sometimes my supervisor puts in deadlines that feel out of my control. (Autonomy)
4. I usually feel competent, but the novel statistical test feels outside of my skill set. (Competency)
5. I hate working in the office because it feels so lonely. (Relatedness)

Your list probably won't look so neat and that's absolutely fine. Just having a list of the problems is a great place to start.

When we are clear on what the problems are, we can go about finding the right solutions to them. That's it for today. Tomorrow, we are going to work on your problem statement.

Day 20
Developing Your Problem Statement (Part 1)

Having identified a list of challenges that impact your motivation, today we will seek further clarity and specificity on your motivational challenge. This will enable us to move into solution mode.

First, look at your initial motivation from your list on Day 19. If your initial motivation for starting your PhD continues to energise you, you can skip this step. Indeed, do skip any part below that is not relevant.

I want you to think about why you are no longer motivated by your doctoral research when you started with this motivation. Is this always the case now, or just in some situations? Think about what has changed. Below is an example of a problem statement describing a change in motivation:

I am no longer motivated by a six-figure salary. My partner is now bringing in most of our income and he is happy for me to pursue other family goals, which is more appealing to me now. However, I don't want to completely give up my thesis. It is important for me to finish this because I want to keep my options open in the future.

> **I invite you to write two to five lines describing this as a problem statement.**

Now, look at your motivational barriers list on Day 19 in relation to your values. How can you expand this? What values previously helped drive your motivation but now do not? What values would you like to drive you going forward? Draft the next component of your statement. It may look like this:

I value novelty, but am no longer experiencing this in my doctoral research. I am currently spending a lot of time writing up my thesis and this involves mainly reporting back on what I have done in the research process. I am therefore not getting much novelty. I value making an impact and this might be a value that could energise me going forward. I also value sharing my research with others and I wonder if this could be something to look forward to.

> **Write two to five lines describing the role of values in a problem statement.**

Finally, I invite you to review your motivational barriers list from yesterday in relation to autonomy.

How is your sense of control impacting your motivation? Is it always like this? Are there some circumstances in which you have more control than other circumstances? Why is this? Expand your statement. For example:

My supervisor puts in deadlines that feel out of my control. She often does this to motivate me, but sometimes it feels like too much of a stretch and I'm tempted to just give up. I often feel anxious about our meetings because I'm worried about what she will say. However, I have control over the time I prepare for these meetings and I could be more assertive in negotiating deadlines with her.

> **Write two to five lines describing the role of autonomy in a problem statement.**

That's enough for today.

Well done! Tomorrow, we're going to finish the problem statement.

Day 21
Developing Your Problem Statement (Part 2)

Yesterday, you started drafting your problem statement. Today, we're going to continue refining and completing this statement. You're nearly at the end of Section 3. Great job!

The first job for today is to review your motivational barriers list on Day 19 in relation to competency. Can you specify the tasks or issues where you experience competency as a problem? Can you explain why this is? Consider whether this is rooted in actual feedback you have received. What strengths do you have that could help you increase your feelings of competence? Your statement might look like this:

Whilst I usually feel competent, I do not know what I'm doing with this novel statistical test. I have a lot of experience in using statistical methods and I teach undergraduates on it - and I feel good about doing this. So, it's not the case that I'm rubbish at statistics. I wonder if I could find a mentor to support me using this method?

> **Write two to five lines describing the role of competency as a problem statement.**

Your next task is to look at relatedness. Review what you identified on Day 19 in your motivational barriers for relatedness. Is it always a barrier? When is it not? Specify the circumstances in which feeling connected is a problem. Can you expand by stating why this is? What does this say about how you could deal with the problem? An example below:

I hate working in the postgrad office. It's freezing and I'm often the only one in there, apart from Wednesdays when everyone comes in. I really value people's company on a Wednesday as we get to share ideas. I usually enjoy working from home and I get to see the kids when they come home from school.

> **Write two to five lines describing the role of relatedness as a problem statement.**

Your last job is to bring these components together to form a detailed problem statement. This could look something like this:

Problem Statement for my Motivational Challenges

I am no longer motivated by a six-figure salary. My partner is now bringing in most of our income and he is happy for me to pursue other family goals, which is more appealing to me now. However, I don't completely want to give up my thesis. It is important for me to finish this because I want to keep my options open in the future.

I value novelty, but am no longer experiencing this in my doctoral research. I am currently spending a lot of time writing up my thesis and this involves mainly reporting back on what I have done in the research process. I am therefore not getting much novelty. I value making an impact and this might be a value that could energise me going forward. I also value sharing my research with others and I wonder if this could be something to look forward to.

My supervisor puts in deadlines that feel out of my control. They often do this to motivate me, but sometimes it feels too much of a stretch and I'm tempted to give up. I often feel anxious about going to our meetings because I'm worried about what my supervisor will say. However, I have control over the time I prepare for these meetings and I could be more assertive in negotiating deadlines with them.

Whilst I usually feel competent, I do not know what I'm doing with this novel statistical test. I have a lot of experience in using statistical methods and I teach undergraduates on it. Indeed, I feel good about my teaching role. So it's not the case that I'm rubbish at statistics. I wonder if I could find a mentor to support me using this method?

I hate working in the postgrad office. It's freezing and I'm often the only one in there, apart from Wednesdays when everyone comes in. I really value people's company on a Wednesday as we get to share ideas. I usually enjoy working from home and I get to see the kids when they return from school.

> **Spend some time compiling the problem statements into one document.**

Good work! I hope this gives you greater clarity on your specific problems. If you need to take a moment to be kind to yourself, do so. Tomorrow, we will start moving towards taking action.

Section 4:
Developing an action plan.

By the end of this section, you will have:
- ✓ Clarified how you will approach your motivational challenges.
- ✓ Classified the type of problems you are dealing with.
- ✓ Developed a range of actions you can choose from.
- ✓ Evaluated the actions you could take.
- ✓ Created a coherent action plan.
- ✓ Considered the potential barriers to implementing your plan.
- ✓ Identified how you will be accountable for achieving your plan.
- ✓ Reflected on how you will celebrate your achievements.

Day 22
Prioritising Action (Part 1)

Hopefully, you found yesterday useful. How does it feel to look at your problem statement? Do you feel relieved it's all in one place? Or perhaps you feel overwhelmed? Take a second to acknowledge your feelings. I hope you have a clearer sense of the issues that are leading you to feel demotivated. You may feel that there are other factors that have not been included. If this is the case, add these in.

Today, we're going to keep it simple and think about priorities. This is a key part of your plan. Having a priority is about being clear on what you are going to deal with first.

I remember working on my PhD a few months before my wedding. I had created a colourful chart, which showed my thesis word count and placed it on my wall. But I felt stressed and my wife-to-be wasn't all that pleased at how I was approaching things!

I remember clearly, her telling me, "Ben, you can't have four different priorities!" If you have a lot of priorities, then you don't have a priority!!

She was totally right.

I couldn't make time to organise the wedding, do my job, look for new accommodation and write my PhD. It was too much. In the end, I took a short period of leave from my doctoral research to plan my wedding. I'm guessing she was glad I chose her over the thesis!

You can't have lots of priorities. You will be more effective if you choose one or two areas to focus on at a time. Of course, this doesn't mean that you can't address all the problem areas. It just means that you won't deal with them all at the same time.

> **Today, I have a simple job for you to do. I want you to think through which is more important to you: (i) Getting a quick win by focusing on one challenge you face; or (ii) Dealing with the issue that has the biggest impact on your motivation. Explain your reasons.**

Have a think and record what you're going to do.

That's it. Good job!

Day 23
Prioritising Action (Part 2)

Let's dive straight into today. You hopefully know whether you want a quick win or a big impact[5]. Of course, you might want both, but at least this gives you a framework to think about prioritising action.

Today, I want you to go through the list of problems in your problem statement and rate them according to their impact on your motivation and how long it will take you to solve. This will give you two scores.

> **Motivation Impact**
> Score each of the problems in your problem statement with a number between 1 to 10 according to how the problems impact your motivation. A score of 1 = low impact on your motivation; a score of 10 = high impact on your motivation.

---

[5] I have offered two ways to rate the problems affecting your motivation which will help you decide which problems to prioritise. If you would rather rate your motivational challenges using a different criteria, by all means do so!

> **Time to Solve**
> **Now score each problem with a *guestimate* of how long it will take you to solve the issue. Again, assign a score between 1 and 10, where**
> **1 = very slow to solve and**
> **10 = very quick to solve.**

Each of the problems listed in the problem statement should have two scores. You also have some clarity on whether you want to deal with the problems to get a high impact or a quick fix (or a combination of both).

I have outlined an example of what this could look like below:

- I have a lack of novelty.
  Motivation - 5; Time to solve – 3.

- Supervisor deadlines feel out of control.
  Motivation - 8; Time to solve – 6.

- Feeling a lack of competence with statistical test.
  Motivation - 9; Time to solve – 3.

- Isolated in the postgrad office.
  Motivation - 6; Time to solve – 7.

> **Your next task is to sort the problems according to the order in which you are going to address them.**

I suggest you use letters rather than numbers to order your list, because you are going to have a lot of numbers on the page from all your scoring. Give the first problem the letter "A"; the next problem, the letter "B" and so on. In the example below, the problems are sorted by how long they will take to solve, with the quickest listed first).

- A - Isolated in postgrad office.
  Motivation – 6; Time to solve – 7.

- B - Supervisor deadlines feel out of control.
  Motivation – 8; Time to solve – 6.

- C - Feeling a lack of competence with statistical test.
  Motivation – 9; Time to solve – 3.

- D - I have a lack of novelty.
  Motivation – 5; Time to solve – 3.

> **Your last task for today is to be clear on what kind of problem you are first dealing with: Is it a problem of competence, autonomy or relatedness?**

This may already be clear. It may not be. Is the first problem you have on your list (which you have assigned as problem "A"), one of competence, autonomy or relatedness? In the example below, feeling isolated is mainly one of relatedness.

- A - Isolated in the postgrad office.
  Motivation – 6; Time to solve – 7.
  Relatedness.

Well done! Tomorrow, we're going to identify some options for dealing with your "A" problem.

Day 24
What Are Your Options?

You've identified your "A" problem and you know what the motivational component is. Today, it's time to think through some questions based on the type of motivational issue in play. By the end of today, you will have some options for dealing with it.

In this chapter, I have provided a worked example for the competency component. This offers a demonstration of how to generate options to solve your motivational problem. I recommend you read this first, even if your motivational issue is not primarily one of competency.

> **Use the questions below to help you generate options for your motivational problem.**

Competency Component Questions
- How realistic is your appraisal of your skill set?
- What would a friend say to you about this?
- Which specific aspects of the problem do you feel are out of your skill set?
- Why is this a problem for you now?

- What is stopping you from finding a way around this? How might a work-around be found?
- Who do you know that could help you deal with this?
- In your ideal world, how would you solve this?
- List your top three options for dealing with this.

Competency Example

To give you an idea of how this can help, let's look at an example of a competency problem statement. You might remember this from Day 21:

"Whilst I usually feel competent, I do not know what I'm doing with this novel statistical test. I have a lot of experience in using statistical methods and I teach undergraduates on it - and I feel good about doing this. So it's not the case that I'm rubbish at statistics. I wonder if I could find a mentor to support me using this method?"

Let's imagine that this issue belongs to Drew, a fictional PhD candidate. He goes through the questions I have listed under competency and thinks about how realistic this appraisal is. He believes there is some truth to it. However, when he thinks about what a friend might say, he notes:

My friend would say, "Drew, you are totally awesome at research methods. You teach so many classes and you've written a review paper on novel methods. Maybe you just need to chat it through with a colleague."

This gives Drew the option of finding a colleague he can discuss his struggles with.

Drew considers the specific aspects of his challenge. He concludes he is struggling with implementing the statistical test in the computer package. The problem is feeling less overwhelming. He knows that there is a helpline for the computer package he uses, so he lists this as another option.

His ideal solution would be to ask his supervisor to solve the problem, but this is not a viable approach! However, what he could do is identify a list of questions to take to his supervisor regarding the computer package and see what ideas they have.

By thinking through some questions, he has arrived at three options:
a) Talk to a colleague about the challenge.
b) Use a search engine to find the software helpline.
c) Compile a list of questions for his supervisor.

Hopefully, this competency example has helped you understand how to generate options for dealing with your motivational challenge. What follows now are specific questions to apply to motivational challenges with autonomy or relatedness components.

Autonomy Component Questions
- What, specifically, feels out of your control about this problem?
- How could you approach this differently to exercise influence or control?
- What would it take to increase your sense of control, even by a moderate amount? How could you make this happen?
- What areas of this work do you feel are within your influence? How could you extend this influence to the problem area?
- Who could help you gain a greater sense of control?
- List your top three options for dealing with this.

Relatedness Component Questions
- When was the last time you felt connected with others in your work?
- What has led to a decrease in connectivity?
- What is stopping you from finding ways to connect with others?
- How might you build connections?

- How do you think your friends might advise you to deal with this?
- What skills do you have that will help you nurture your relationships?
- Who could support you to take your first steps?
- List your top three options for dealing with this.

Make sure that you have written several viable options for dealing with the problem. This will give you room to evaluate them tomorrow.

As ever, if going through these questions is emotionally challenging for you, take some time out and be kind to yourself. Find the support you need.

Good job for today.

Day 25
Review Your Options

You're nearly at the end of this 28-day programme. Well done for getting this far. If you worked on yesterday's task, you should have three options for dealing with your specific motivational challenge.

Today, we are going to evaluate the options you have identified. You may feel this is an unnecessary step. If you have clearly arrived at three simple options to get you off the ground, then fine, skip this step! However, it's possible that you've found yourself stuck because the situation is more complex and needs clear thinking and a plan.

Evaluating your options can provide you with clarity as to how you take things forward.

How are we going to evaluate your options? First, think through how easy each of these options will be to implement. Have a think about how much energy and effort will be needed. Do you want to put in this effort? What resources will your options require? Do you have these resources to hand?

> **Score each option from 1 to 10, where 1 is very difficult and 10 is very easy to implement.**

Second, consider how effective each option is likely to be. What is your gut telling you? What evidence do you have regarding how likely the option is to succeed? Given the skills and resources available to you, what might this say about the likely success and effectiveness?

> **Score each option from 1 to 10, where 1 is not likely to be effective and 10 is highly likely to be effective.**

That's it. See you tomorrow!

Day 26
Putting Together a Plan

Just three more days to go!

Today, it's time to put together a plan. You have briefly evaluated your options and this should give you a sense of which ideas to try first.

Your problem statement will probably contain several motivational components, each of which may need their own set of options. I therefore want to acknowledge that what you have likely arrived at is one set of options for one motivational component. However, in this process, I encouraged you to select a single issue - the one that is quickest to solve or that would have the highest impact on your motivation. This is in recognition that you cannot prioritise everything.

Part of your plan might be to schedule a time to go back to the other parts of your problem statement and develop options for dealing with these problems at a different time.

If, however, you decide you want your plan to encompass all aspects of your problem statement, you can choose to spend time now repeating the process of identifying your options, evaluating these options, and integrating them into a plan.

> **Your initial step is to decide which option from Day 25 you wish to use as a solution.**

Having selected this option, set out the problem component and the proposed option/solution like the example below from Drew:

I usually feel competent, but I do not know what I'm doing with this novel statistical test. My preferred option is to compile a list of questions for my supervisor.

This is a good start to Drew's plan. Next, we want to break this down into some actionable steps, with a deadline for each step. What are the actions that need to happen for this option to be implemented? For instance:

1) *I need to arrange a time to meet with my supervisor. I'm going to email them today and request a meeting at their earliest free slot. (Deadline: Today).*
2) *I need to sit down and just write out the issues and questions that I have. (Deadline: Four days' time).*
3) *I need to attend the meeting and put these questions to my supervisor. (Deadline: At meeting - make note in the diary to chase supervisor).*

> **Break your option down into actions and put a deadline next to each action.**

Next, consider if there are any barriers that might stop you from achieving this plan. What might go wrong? Is there anything you need to consider doing to make sure all goes to plan? Drew considers:

a) *I might be too tired to sit down and write out my questions in two days as I've got a conference presentation due in. I'm going to set a reminder in my diary to make sure I write out these questions after the presentation is done.*
b) *My supervisor isn't always great at responding to my requests, so I'm going to set a reminder to chase him.*

> **Identify the potential barriers for each action.**

Finally, how will you know you have achieved this plan and addressed the problem? What will the outcome look like? What would you be happy achieving? In Drew's example, his outcome looks like this:

In two weeks' time, I will have a simple plan that details how I will carry out this novel statistical test.

> **Describe your ideal outcomes.**

If Drew does not achieve this outcome in two weeks, he is going to revisit some of the other options he thought of. What will you do if your plan misses the mark? (Giving up is not allowed!).

> **Your final task is to identify alternative, contingency actions as part of your plan.**

Phew! You're nearly there. Tomorrow, we will explore how you can use accountability to make your plan happen.

Day 27
Finding Accountability

Welcome! Two days to go. If you've not written out your plan, now is the time to do so. Writing it down helps to make it concrete. It may also give you a bit more head space, as you're not having to retain the plan in your head.

Today, I'd like you to think about how you can keep yourself accountable.

Accountability can provide you with the motivation to action the task and keep to the deadline you set. It's not about giving yourself a hard time if you don't succeed: Don't use accountability to beat yourself up!

I know that when I set a goal for myself at work, it's much easier to find the motivation to do this when I have agreed it with my boss and I know when I'm next meeting them. I make sure the task gets done before I meet them so I can tell them what I have achieved. If the goal is just a repetitive reminder in my office calendar, it's easy to hit snooze and ignore it. Without the accountability and the motivation, too often the goal lacks the priority to get my attention and the action to get it done.

What does accountability look like to you? Is it asking a friend or colleague to check-in with you about the plan you've put together? Perhaps it's about setting a big reminder in your diary to review your progress? I once came across a life coach who put all his own goals and progress on his website - a very public form of accountability!

> **Your job today is to put in place some form of accountability - a way of ensuring you or someone else will follow up and review the progress you have made towards the plan.**

That's it for today!

Day 28
Celebration

You did it! Congratulations on reaching the end of the 28-day plan. I hope you've found it useful.

Today, I encourage you to make space to review and celebrate the progress you have made. How are you feeling about getting on with your doctoral work?

More hopeful?

More energised?

In some respects, it's still early days. You have identified the problem leading to your reduced motivation, you've taken steps to understand the options available to you, and you've put together a plan with a deadline and some accountability. Today is not about expecting you to have achieved everything. Today is about acknowledging the work you have put in to get to where you are.

One of the biggest gifts that coaching can give you is the gift of insight. Coaching provides people with a space to explore what is going on and attain clarity on their challenges. How people use these insights is up to them.

> **I wonder, what have you learnt about yourself over the last four weeks?
> How will this help you in the future?**

What have you learnt about your motivational difficulties? And motivation, more broadly? How can your learning help you with your doctoral research - and with other life challenges?

Finally, how can you celebrate the work you have put in over the last 28 days? What will you do to acknowledge this work? Celebrations can be an important way to acknowledge things that are important to us. They can be as big or as small as you want.

Simple ways that I use to celebrate include treating myself to extra cream or syrup in my coffee; buying a dine-in-for-two meal; grabbing a takeaway. You can see that all my celebration examples involve food: Perhaps you have other ways to celebrate? Whatever works for you, take a moment to plan how you will acknowledge your progress.

> **Make sure you do something concrete to celebrate your achievements!**

I'd love to hear how you have found this book.

Drop me a message info@coachingacademics.co.uk and visit my website www.coachingacademics.co.uk to discover how coaching can help you.

If you would value more support and accountability, then life coaching may be for you.

Finally, I wish you all the best with progressing your thesis. Hold on to the progress you've made to date and use this as an encouragement to keep persevering. You can totally do this!

Dr. Benjamin Newton

Acknowledgments

A huge thank you is warranted to all the beta-readers and reviewers who helped add the final touches to this book.

Some of them have requested to stay anonymous - but huge thanks go to you all.

Thank you to Zoë Bell, Sharon Newson, Juan Rivera, Dr. Eric Saboya, Dr. Vishal Sharma and Sarah Turner for all the helpful suggestions and feedback. A huge thanks also to the coaches I have spoken to who have provided me pearls of wisdom as I have shared this book with them.

And finally, a big thank you to my family who have supported me on this writing journey.

www.ingramcontent.com/pod-product-compliance
Lightning Source LLC
Chambersburg PA
CBHW071403080526
44587CB00017B/3162